Feasts and Festivals

Feasts and Festivals

a celebration of Pacific Island culture in New Zealand

Glenn Jowitt

text by Graeme Lay

NEW HOLLAND

Feasts and Festivals Contents

This book is dedicated to all my friends
in the Pacific

Preface

During the 20 years I have been working with various Pacific Island communities, both here in Auckland and in their homelands, I have experienced a level of trust and acceptance that is ongoing to this day. The love and assistance extended to me has allowed me the access I needed to undertake various projects over the years, most recently the work portrayed in this book.

My involvement in the Polynesian community goes back to when I was growing up in the Hutt Valley. Then, when I moved to Auckland as an adult, I was attracted to my Pacific Island neighbours – they exuded great warmth towards me and I loved their natural sense of colour and celebration.

Some time after that I undertook further studies in the United States, during which time I began to understand the long-term effects of the 1950s and '60s Pacific Island migrations to Auckland on New Zealand's cultural fabric. (By 1980 Auckland was the biggest Polynesian city in the world.) On my return to Auckland I could see that documenting some aspects of local Pacific Island communities was the obvious progression of my work.

As this project evolved, invitations to the homelands were extended to me and it became inevitable that I would make my way to some of the islands. With the assistance of Anna Louise Van Rooyen, an anthropology graduate, not only was I able to travel to the Cooks, Niue, Tokelau, Samoa and Tonga, I was also able to stay with the families of friends. This hospitality made it possible for me to work at the very heart of each community.

Out of these travels grew the 1983 exhibition 'Polynesia Here and There' and the subsequent catalogue, *Pacific Images*, in 1986, 10 children's books and, more recently, *Pacific Island Style*, which was a finalist in the Lifestyle category of the 2000 Montana New Zealand Book Awards.

Documenting the unique cultural activities at the heart of Auckland's Pacific Island communities over the years has been a great privilege. It has also allowed me to give something back to these peoples who have been so caring, generous and understanding of the work I have attempted to do. *Feasts and Festivals* is a continuation of this documentary photography and, like my previous work, it has been a wonderful experience.

Glenn Jowitt

Introduction

Cook Islands drumming team at the Pasifika Festival, Western Springs, Auckland. The trio of cylindrical slit drums, called pate, are made by hollowing out lengths of wood, which are struck at terrific speed with turned sticks. The bass drum (right) is covered in stretched goatskin and beaten with a sturdy drum stick. Cook Island drummers are considered the finest in the South Pacific.

Above all, the bold, primary colours of the South Pacific have brightened up New Zealand: blues, greens, reds and golds, reflecting the hue of the world's largest ocean, the lush vegetation and the flowers, the brightness of the tropical sun. This love of colour is so strong within Pacific Island peoples that it is transplanted to wherever they live. And so in New Zealand's South Pacific communities, accompanying their festivals, ceremonies and dances, bright colours are ubiquitous. A garland of scented frangipani flowers, a hibiscus bloom behind the ear, a lavalava patterned in shades of purple and gold, an applique quilt of green and blue – the effect of colours like these is striking and immediate, livening up an otherwise temperate land and recalling those sun-drenched islands of the South Pacific.

Yet the colourful adornments and decor so loved by South Pacific peoples are merely the trappings of celebration. Beneath the costumes, flowers and other embellishments are deeply significant, traditional ceremonies which are an integral part of the cultural luggage Pacific Island peoples brought with them to New Zealand, and which have been retained by the generations born and raised here. These include religious observances, songs, dances and traditional rites of passage.

This book is a showcase for these vibrant South Pacific festivities, many of which have become an integral part of New Zealand's urban life, particularly in Auckland, now truly the world's largest Polynesian city.

The story of how these South Pacific festivities were transplanted to New Zealand begins on the scores of scattered high islands and atolls which comprise tropical Polynesia, in the Cook Islands, Niue Island, Samoa, the Tokelau Islands and Tonga. This is the region of the south-west Pacific, the area that was also the ancient homeland of New Zealand's indigenous people, the Maori.

These first New Zealanders, skilled ocean voyagers from the islands of eastern Polynesia, discovered the islands which came to be called by them Aotearoa in about AD 1000. Physically very different to the tropical, reef-girdled islands they had left behind and huge by comparison and climatically temperate, this unfamiliar land's differences forced the first Polynesian immigrants to adopt new methods of hunting, fishing, food gathering and preparation, crop growing and building. They adapted successfully, cultivating new crops to replace the tropical ones which would not grow in the cooler climate, and crafting their tools, garments and dwellings from different materials. Their adaptation was so successful that within 500 years the descendants of those original Polynesian immigrants had settled the islands of Aotearoa from their sub-tropical far north to the cool south. A distinctive Maori culture evolved, related to but different in many respects from that of the South Pacific islands which their forbears had left.

European colonisation of New Zealand in the 19th century brought radical changes to every aspect of traditional Maori society, but again the people adapted to new ways of living. The Maori race, predicted by many to die out, proved resilient in the face of change, and survived. Over the same period – the second half of the 19th century – nearly all the islands of the South Pacific also came within the ambit of expansionist European Empires: British, French and German. Changes to traditional Pacific Island society were drastic and swift: to religious practices, language, dress codes and settlement patterns. In just decades the way of life in the Islands was transformed.

Of the many fundamental changes European colonisation brought, the most profound were those wrought by the variously denominated Christian missionaries. The Bible became the guiding light throughout the South Pacific. The traditional gods were extirpated, nudity and traditional dancing banned, alcohol prohibited, and customs like tattooing proscribed. Sunday became sacrosanct, the other Christian anniversaries strictly observed. The Church became the overriding authority. Whether Roman Catholic, Wesleyan or Church of England, the effect was the same: throughout the South Pacific traditional culture was suppressed.

But centuries of culture and custom could not be eradicated so easily, in spite of missionary zeal. The milestones of life's journey – birth, puberty, marriage and death – which had always been accompanied by time-honoured ritual in the Pacific Islands, were adapted to Christian lore. The old gods were not quite forgotten, the places of traditional worship, the maraes, not entirely destroyed. Myths and legends continued to be passed down orally from one generation to the next; dancing and drumming were suppressed rather than eliminated, and the custom of feasting was upheld. The number of festivities actually increased, as Christian anniversaries were added to the calendar. In Tonga the ceremonial preparation and drinking of the indigenous beverage, kava, was encouraged by the Church, whose authorities deemed it preferable to alcohol consumption.

Pacific garlands are a form of wearable art. The strong love that Pacific Island people have for flowers, bright colours and decoration finds expression in their weaving and wearing of garlands, which are worn on any occasion, formal or informal.

Hair-cutting and ear-piercing ceremonies – important rites of passage for pubescent children in Niue and the Cook Islands – were given an overlay of Christianity, while special Christian celebrations like White Sunday became highly significant occasions in Samoa, the Tokelaus and Tonga.

Political developments in the early 20th century turned New Zealand's attention towards the islands of the South Pacific. In 1901, driven by a dream of imperial grandeur, the New Zealand Government annexed the 15 islands of the Cook group, then Niue Island. Thirteen years later, upon the outbreak of World War I, New Zealand troops were despatched to the then-German colony of Western Samoa and quickly assumed rule over those islands. The atolls of the Tokelau group also came under New Zealand jurisdiction at this time. In the south-west Pacific region, only the Kingdom of Tonga was not subjected to direct colonial rule by New Zealand, although as a British Protectorate it was part of the British Empire and as such was informally connected to New Zealand, its nearest 'British' neighbour. The consequences of these developments were far-reaching.

When Western Samoa eventually achieved self-rule in 1962 it was accompanied by a Treaty of Friendship with New Zealand, the former colonial ruler. The Cook Islands (1965) and Niue (1974) both became independent 'in free association with New Zealand', while the remote Tokelaus were administered from Wellington until 1994. This meant that Cook Islanders, Niueans and Tokelauans had free right of entry into New Zealand after independence, while the Western Samoans, although subject to more stringent entry regulations, were able to apply to immigrate to New Zealand on a quota basis. A stricter quota system applied to the people of Tonga and Fiji.

The high islands of Polynesia are sublimely beautiful. Verdant and well-watered, islands such as Rarotonga in the Cook Islands and Upolu in Samoa have fertile valleys and coastal plains, bountiful lagoons and mountain cores covered in stands of rainforest. The rich, volcanic soil sustains tropical crops like taro, breadfruit and bananas; the surrounding sea teems with fish. But these high islands are vastly outnumbered by low islands, or atolls, the sunken remains of once-high, ancient volcanoes, slivers of coral rock and sand encircling wide lagoons. The six islands of the Northern Group of the Cook Islands are atolls, as are all the Tokelau Islands and most of the islands of Tonga. Niue is an atoll which has been raised high above sea level.

On the low islands there is no natural soil, no streams or rivers, no deposit of useful minerals such as coal or iron ore. Life on an atoll is hard, its inhabitants depending on the sea and a few staple food crops such as coconuts and bananas. Other foods must be imported, along with costly fuel for outboard motors and power generators, as well as freezers, vehicles and other consumer goods. Natural hazards such as cyclones and droughts hover just over the horizon.

In the 1960s and 1970s, throughout the atolls and high islands of the South Pacific, demographic pressures were building. Improved health care had virtually wiped out formerly endemic diseases

The face of today's Auckland. A Pacific Island-New Zealand girl wearing a blend of Pacific fashion and traditional head adornment. The Pacific Island population is a youthful one, today mostly New Zealand-born.

Rarotongan hats have both aesthetic and functional appeal. Hand-woven from the young middle frond of the coconut palm, the hats are worn by women on all formal occasions.

A garland of frangipani blooms and vine leaves crowns a Pacific Island woman.

Colourful head adornment is not exclusive to Pacific Island women; men too have a love of colour and embellishment and customarily decorate their heads with natural or artificial flowers. Here a man shows off his vivid millinery.

Dyed feathers make a flamboyant fashion accessory. Pacific Islanders are highly adaptable people who now incorporate a variety of synthetic materials into headwear and costumes, a necessary adaptation when tropical flowers are not available in temperate New Zealand.

Tongan boys ready to perform their items at the Auckland Secondary Schools Maori and Pacific Islands Cultural Festival, 1993. Although the material for the boys' costumes is synthetic, their dances will be entirely traditional and marked according to rigorous cultural standards by a panel of judges selected for their deep knowledge of Tongan culture.

Only minutes to go: pre-performance tension shows in the faces of these
young Tongan group members before they go on stage at the festival.
Inter-school competition is intense. The judges award marks for criteria
such as punctuality, costumes, performance and discipline, and the results
of their judgement are awaited keenly on the last day of the festival.

such as smallpox, filariasis and leprosy. Vaccination reduced infant mortality, life expectancy increased and the islands, with their already high birth rates, began to experience rapid population growth, increasing the pressure on limited land resources, education and health services. Even on the high islands, there was little industry, few employment opportunities and very low wage rates. For those who wanted a better and more prosperous life for themselves and their children, the solution was emigration.

From the 1960s onwards, many people in the south-west Pacific began to look southwards to New Zealand, where in the cities secondary and tertiary industries were growing rapidly and there was an urgent demand for labour which could not be supplied locally. New Zealand thus offered opportunities the islands never could: relatively well paid factory or service sector work, higher education, better health care and a way of life more varied and rewarding for their families.

Emigration took the form of a classic 'chain migration' movement. A family would make the brave decision to leave their village on, say, Aitutaki in the Cook Islands, Savaii in Samoa or Tongatapu in Tonga, save the airfares required and move to Auckland or Wellington, then report their success, thus encouraging others to follow. In this way the out-migration trickle from the Pacific Islands became a flow, then a flood. In the case of Niue, entire villages flew away, wrote back and encouraged the rest to uproot themselves. The results are dramatic: today there are only 1200 people left on 'The Rock', as they call Niue, while 18,500 Niueans live in New Zealand. There are 16,000 people living in the Cook Islands, 48,000 people of Cook Island ethnicity in New Zealand; 160,000 people in Samoa, and over 100,000 Samoans in New Zealand. Overall, in 1951 there were only 3600 Pacific Islanders living in New Zealand. By 1961 the figure had risen to 14,300; by 1971 to 43,700; by 1981 to nearly 94,000 and by 1996 it had reached just under 217,000. Today the Pacific Island population is approaching a quarter of a million.

The South Pacific migrants brought with them their distinctive cultures, which were resilient enough to survive the colonial period and were resurrected with new pride after independence. In New Zealand too these cultures were maintained, partly as a comfort and reminder of home for the immigrants, then instilled in the second and third generations by the older people, who were determined that their traditional way of life would not be lost in the new land. Dance, song, drumming, worship and rites of passage were all retained, adding diversity and colour to New Zealand society, where previously only the Maori traditional cultural dances, songs and ceremonies had leavened the predominantly British heritage. Polynesian celebrations like Auckland's Pasifika and the Secondary Schools Maori and Pacific Islands Cultural Festival began tentatively, then grew dramatically until they are now highlights on the city's events calendar.

Traditionally, Polynesians have a love of formal ceremony, of pomp, speech-making, song, dance and feasting. This is the way it has always been, and the way it will always be, whether the festivities take place in Apia or Otara, Mangaia or Mangere, Avarua or Otahuhu. Prayer, speech, costume, song, dance, food and drink: all are time-honoured elements of Polynesian culture, and as such were an integral part of the traditions which the island immigrants brought with them to New Zealand. With Polynesian weddings, funerals, christenings and coming-of-age celebrations, no expense is spared, no guest list can be too long. The ceremony is time-honoured, the formalities pronounced, the catering lavish. Respect, pride and dignity, all are palpable throughout these observances.

Nor are such celebrations merely a passing phase, for the New Zealand of the future will become more of a South Pacific nation than ever. By the year 2051 it is estimated that Polynesian people – Maori and Pacific Islanders – will comprise 30 percent of New Zealand's total population, almost double what it is today. In 1996 Pacific Island people made up just 6 percent of New Zealand's population, but with a high birth rate increasing their numbers by 3.3 percent annually – over twice that of the growth rate for the Pakeha population – this proportion will double, to 12 percent, within half a century, thus providing a much higher profile for Pacific cultures and people. Forty percent of the Pacific Island population is under 15 years of age, thus ensuring a continued high birth rate. Combined with an increasing proportion of Maori people – to about 18 percent – the predicted total of a 30 percent Polynesian population appears realistic.

The fact that 60 percent of all Pacific Islanders in this country are now New Zealand-born has not greatly reduced their adherence to their families' traditional culture and customs. Most maintain strong ties with their extended families in the Islands, while younger generations are reminded of their heritage by their parents and grandparents. Many second and third-generation Pacific Islanders have a sound understanding of their traditional language. Nor has intermarriage with Pakeha New Zealanders – now a common occurrence in urban society – diluted Pacific Island culture. The children of such marriages usually identify more strongly with their Polynesian heritage than with their Pakeha side, mainly because their Island culture is more tangible and readily expressed.

The Church remains the hoop of iron which holds the communities together and sustains the community and its culture. There are few other people as devout as Pacific Islanders, and their churches, as well as forming the core of their communities, are striking landmarks in our cities and suburbs. Christian beliefs are instilled in the young through rigorous church attendance and special festivals such as White Sunday, when children are honoured by the church and their families. The dedication of a new church, achieved after concerted community fund-raising, is an occasion of great celebration and ceremony.

Two-thirds of New Zealand's Pacific Island people live in Auckland, a city which consequently now has an unmistakable South Pacific ambience. Pacific art, design, music and fashion – particularly that of the ubiquitous tapa designs – is firmly established. The striking work of artists like Fatu Feu'u, Lily Laiti, Michel Tuffery, Ani O'Neil, Dagmar Dyck, Jim Vivieaere and Filipe Tohi enhances our public buildings and galleries. Bold Pacific colours in décor are fashionable, while on the music scene the rhythms of the South Seas, first made popular as early as the 1950s by groups like Bill Wolfgramm and his Islanders, are increasingly part of the mainstream music scene.

In sport Pacific Islanders excel, and, like Maori players, are strongly represented in New Zealand's rugby, league and netball teams. Pacific Island All Black greats include Bryan Williams, Michael Jones, Frank Bunce, Olo Brown, Jonah Lomu and Tana Umaga; while Silver Ferns legends Rita Fatialofa, April Ieremia, Bernice Mene and Margharet Matenga are all from Pacific Island families. And these are just the superstars – Pacific Islanders are heavily over-represented in proportion to their numbers in the elite ranks of Super 12 and NPC rugby and national netball competitions. David Tua, a Samoan New Zealander, has risen to the highest rank of heavyweight boxing, Beatrice Faumuina to the summit of international athletics. In summer the public parks of Auckland resound to the whack of rubber against wood as kilikiti, the Samoan and Niuean version of that most English of sports – cricket, is played with enormous rivalry, gusto and exuberance.

A green room with a difference. Ignoring the writing on the wall, Cook Islands women add the finishing touches to their appearance before taking the stage at Ponsonby's 'Gluepot' hotel, in 1992. Cook Islands cultural groups provide a very popular form of entertainment at many Auckland nightspots. Their dancing and drumming displays are now appreciated in many other parts of the world.

De La Salle's Tongan Group in full swing with their
war dance, called the kailao, at the Auckland Secondary
Schools Maori and Pacific Islands Cultural Festival.

Because the Pacific Island population is overwhelmingly urban, the New Zealand-born children are raised, educated and socialise in the city. Theirs is a world of shopping malls and supermarkets, video parlours and mobile phones, McDonald's and money machines. It might be expected that this generation, worldly and streetwise, has left its Island heritage far behind, but in fact the culture of its parents and grandparents is far from repudiated. Pride in traditional customs and language is passed to the New Zealand-born generations through the extended family, church and youth groups, sports teams and, on special occasions, through their schools' cultural groups.

The Auckland Secondary Schools Maori and Pacific Islands Cultural Festival is now one of the biggest events on the school calendar. Held in late March and since 1995 at the Manukau Sports Bowl, the three-day festival has grown at a tremendous rate from its inception at Hillary College, Otara, in 1976. Today over 150 cultural groups from 50 schools – from Asian cultures now as well as the South Pacific, reflecting Auckland's increasing multiculturalism – take part in the festival, in both competitive and non-competitive sections, and it is attended by 100,000 people from all age groups. The venue lies directly beneath the flight path to Auckland International Airport, and flights from the South Pacific regularly descend over the Sports Bowl, in so doing following the path that many people have followed over the past three decades from the Pacific Islands to Auckland City. Beneath the flight path, spread across the undulations of the grassy reserve, are the five cultural performance stages, along with stalls selling Island foods: banana poke, taro chips, mussels in coconut cream, pisupo (corned beef), chop suey, koko Samoa, drinking coconuts, banana pancakes and watermelon. The tastes as well as the sounds of the South Pacific are to be sampled at the young people's cultural festival.

For Maori and Pacific Island youth the festival is not only a hugely enjoyable social occasion, it provides them with a platform to perform song and dance to the highest possible standards and in so doing uphold their cultural heritage. The five well-spaced stages represent Maori, Cook Island, Niuean, Samoan and Tongan cultures, and to witness the young people's performances is to realise that something extraordinary is happening here, along with the song and dance fiesta, because the performers also show the changing face of Auckland. Most of the participants, naturally, are Polynesian, but there is an increasing proportion of Pakeha New Zealanders who are also caught up with the verve of the dance performance groups. For example, the Epsom Girls' Grammar School Cook Islands Group, drawn from a school whose students are predominantly white or Asian, dances with no less exuberance and delight, although its participants must constitute the palest Cook Islands dancers in the world. But among them are the small minority of girls who obviously are from Island families, leading their papa'a (European) sisters in the dance, and in so doing transmitting not only their culture but understanding and the tolerance that will flow from it. A Croatian student twirling pois in a Maori group, an Indian student performing the Sasa in a Samoan group, a Palagi student in a Niuean group: this cultural cross-fertilisation must have positive benefits in a city growing more multicultural by the month.

In just a decade, the Pasifika Festival, held on the first Saturday in March at Western Springs Reserve in central Auckland, has grown enormously in scale and popularity. This festival too is a celebration of Pacific Island culture, art and cuisine, and now draws an audience of over 100,000. Eight 'cultural villages', each representing a South Pacific nation, become the focus for their islands' song, dance and customs: Aotearoa, the Cook Islands, Fiji, Niue, Samoa, Tonga, Tokelau and Tuvalu. Dozens of food stalls sell traditional delicacies such as chop suey, pisupo, pawpaw and pineapple and raw

String trio. Island ukeleles may be carved and decorated in different shapes and styles, but their lilting tunes are an essential part of the accompaniment to most South Pacific songs, dances and celebrations.

fish in coconut cream, as well as more commonplace Kiwi kai such as sausages and hot dogs. The Pacific beverage, kava, is prepared in wooden bowls and served in accordance with traditional ceremony. Artwork on display includes garlands and flaxwork, tapa cloth and jewellery such as shell necklaces.

Amid the greenery of the park, the festival-goers and participants present a South Pacific palette of colour as they crowd the pathways around the reserve's main lake. At the eastern end of the reserve are the petrified remains of lava flows which poured from Mt Eden, several kilometres away, 8000 years ago. The jointed lava rock, resembling abstract sculpture, is also a reminder that Auckland lies within the zone of volcanic activity surrounding the Pacific Ocean. In this way Auckland City is connected geologically with the islands of the Pacific, which were themselves born from volcanic eruptions. As well as reinforcing that ancient connection, the annual Pasifika Festival at Western Springs Reserve is also one of the most colourful events on Auckland's cultural programme.

A weekly rather than an annual South Pacific event takes place in the centre of Otara, in South Auckland. Here every Saturday the Otara Market is held, an open air bazaar and entertainment centre begun by Pacific Island people in the 1980s which has grown to become an enormous, multicultural institution. In the Islands the market is a regular, time-honoured event, a central place where fresh produce and other goods are sold cheaply by local people. As a place where people congregate purposefully, the market also has a vital social function. The Otara Market fulfils all these traditional roles: fruit, vegetables, fish, meat and takeaway foods are sold by stall-holders, many now Asian as well as Polynesian (or 'noodles' and 'coconuts' in the local parlance). The

Young dancer from Kiribase,
the Kiribati Community Group.

market offers a mélange of Pacific and Kiwi foods: fresh bananas, mangoes, taro leaves, coconuts and yams are on sale, alongside stalls offering chop suey, pork and puha, hamburgers, hot dogs and doughnuts. There are stalls selling fashion clothing, indigenous T-shirts, tapes and CDs and second-hand goods, while on the margins live performers entertain market-goers with the distinctively Pacific Island music for which Otara has become renowned. There is no better example of how the South Pacific has come to Auckland than Otara's vibrant, multi-ethnic Saturday market.

In 1950 the New Zealand writer M K Joseph published a satiric poem entitled 'Secular Litany'. It was a lament for New Zealand's lack of carnivals and colour. Among its lines, intended to be intoned like a church litany, are those that demand with heavy irony:

> That we may avoid distinction and exception… Worship the mean, cultivate the mediocre…
> From all foreigners, with their unintelligible cooking
> From the vicious habit of public enjoyment
> From kermesse and carnival, high day and festival.
> Defend us.

Over half a century on, the need for such supplication has long passed. New Zealand's urban way of life has been transformed in a way that the poet could not have imagined: festivals and carnivals abound, food, wine, song and dance from scores of different ethnic groups enrich and enliven society. And of the groups, none is more visible, exuberant or colourful than those from the islands of the South Pacific. This book is a celebration of the festivities of these people, and the colour they have brought into all our lives.

A Samoan kava ceremony, an integral part of most Pacific Island ceremonial occasions, taking place at the Pasifika Festival, Western Springs, Auckland (right).

An image of the 'Tua Man', heavyweight boxer David Tua, adorns a stall selling corned beef at the Pasifika Festival (below). Corned beef – known as pisupo – is a popular food throughout the Pacific Islands and in New Zealand's island communities, while David Tua is one of the most famous exports of the country of his birth, Samoa.

Tongan handicrafts such as fans, mats and book covers on
display (below) at the Pasifika Festival, which is an opportunity
for all South Pacific communities to present their cultures to the
Auckland population as a whole. On the day of the festival a
Niuean stall (right) becomes a centre for a family gathering,
with guitar accompaniment, as well as for the sale of handicrafts.

A Royal Event
Dedication of a **Tongan Church**

First Christianised by Wesleyan (Methodist) missionaries from the 1820s onwards, Tonga later became one of the most devout nations in the Pacific. Tonga's constitution, drafted by a Methodist missionary, Shirley Baker, in 1875, declares the Sabbath a sacred day. Even today it is unlawful to work, trade or hold sporting fixtures on Sunday in Tonga, and church attendances are very high. The dominant branch of Christianity remains the Free Wesleyan Church, to which the Tongan royal family and all members of the nobility belong. Tongan expatriate communities also cling fast to their Christian faith, so that the dedication of a new church is an event of deep spiritual and community significance, a time for giving thanks, for fund-raising and for celebrating through song, dance and feasting. The exquisite decorated church cake (opposite), a gift for the king, faithfully embodies this spirit of devotion and celebration and honours the old church, demolished to make way for the construction of the new church.

The present King of Tonga, His Majesty King Taufa'ahau Tupou IV, is a revered figure both within the kingdom and in Tongan overseas communities, so it was a momentous day when His Majesty travelled to New Zealand to dedicate a new church, Vaine Mo'onia ('The True Vine') in Grey Lynn, Auckland, on 29 October 1994. The king was accompanied by his wife, Queen Halaevalu, and the granddaughter of the Premier of Tonga. The ceremony not only marked the beginning of the construction of Vaine Mo'onia, it was a time for giving thanks and expressing the congregation's deep respect for the king's presence at the occasion. Six decorated pigs were presented to the king, in tribute to him, along with other traditional gifts such as fine mats. The significance of the event can also be judged by the fact that 5000 people attended the feast to celebrate the dedication, which was held in the grounds of St Paul's College, Grey Lynn. On the day of the dedication, $80,000 was collected for the church-building project, the total cost of which was $3.1 million.

King Taufa'ahau Tupou IV, sovereign of the Kingdom of Tonga, about to address his people at the dedication of the new Grey Lynn church, with his nephew, the Hon Kalaniuvalu, assisting at the microphone. At right, the King helps lay the church's foundations.

The King speaking from the pulpit at the dedication of the new church (top). Queen Halaevalu is in the background.
His Majesty enters the new church through a portal of fine mats (left).

Fe'ofa'aki Tukino and Makeleta Tukino proudly unveil a cake model of the new church, Vaine Mo'onia, for display at the dedication. Churches such as this one have become distinctive Auckland landmarks, and indicators of the devoutness of the Tongan people.

Young Tongan beauties in traditional costume.
Their skin is covered in coconut oil, which as well as
adding lustre to their bodies, enables the monetary
donations to stay attached as they perform their
dances for the crowd.

Granddaughter of the Premier of Tonga, Atu'amua
Vaea performs the Ta'longa during the dedication
ceremony, to the delight of the older dancers.
The little girl also provides the spark of enthusiasm
for the next vitally important part of the day, the
fund-raising.

The presentation of fine mats by women of the community, in appreciation of the King's attendance at the ceremony. Me'a'ofa – the giving of gifts – is a crucial part of such ceremonial occasions, and fine mats are highly prized. Made from the dried and closely woven leaves of the hardy pandanus plant, which grows everywhere in the tropical South Pacific, the mats are the result of many hours of laborious work by the Tongan women. A gift of six large pigs was also presented to the King. Later these were cut up and distributed among Tongan college students.

The feast accompanying the dedication is laid out. Feasting is extremely important at any Tongan celebration, and roast pigs are the centrepiece of any feast. Fish, fruit, chicken and salad are the other key ingredients of the banquet. A crowd of 5000 attended and feasted at the dedication of Vaine Mo'onia, and on the day of the launch $80,000 was collected, to help pay for the church project.

Dressed for the chilly Auckland weather, matriarchs (left to right) Maluhola, Soloi and Amelia are given pride of place at the feast. Elderly women are accorded high status in Tongan society. No woman was more revered than the present king's mother, Queen Salote, who ruled Tonga from 1918 until her death in 1965.

Blessed are the Children
White Sunday in the Samoan Community

The second Sunday in October is a day of tremendous importance in Samoan communities. Called White Sunday, it is the day of the year when the children of the community – those aged from about two years to 17 years – are honoured by their church and their extended families. The Samoan name for the day is Lotu Tamaiti. White Sunday is also celebrated by the Tongan and Tokelauan communities, although there are significant differences between the cultures in the way the day is marked.

Samoan children prepare for White Sunday many weeks in advance. Part of their regular Sunday School programme, the preparation includes rehearsing a short play, a verse recitation, a sermon or a choral performance. Practices are held after Sunday School in the weeks leading up to the big day in October, and anxiety levels rise as the day itself approaches. Everyone is aware that the children will be on display and it is essential that the highest standards of performance and dress are maintained.

In the morning the children assemble at the church, the girls dressed entirely in white, the boys in white shirts and black trousers or lavalavas. The young people line up outside the church, then at 9 o'clock they file inside, where their parents are already seated. Once seated, within the church there is an air of nervous anticipation among the children (right) at the Congregational Christian Church of Samoa, Grey Lynn, Auckland. The children sing a special hymn, starting with the pre-schoolers and working up to those of Bible Class age. There are prayers, Bible readings, the giving of thanks and saying sorry for any wrongdoings that may have occurred, before a sermon is delivered by one of the older children. After each group performs a hymn is sung, then the plays, verses and songs continue. All the performances are in Samoan, thus helping to maintain the young people's fluency in the language so that it is passed on to the New Zealand-born generation.

The formal part of White Sunday ends with a church elder thanking the children and their parents, before the service concludes with a blessing. Following the service the children return to their homes, where they enjoy a special meal with their parents, brothers and sisters. Then, later in the day, everyone returns to their church's social centre for a communal feast which continues into the evening, until 8 pm or later. Eagerly anticipated by children and parents alike in the Samoan community, White Sunday is a time of excitement, devotion and celebration. Truly, a day for the children.

Dressed immaculately for their big day (top), the youngest children are led into the church by Sunday School teachers Fono Tigafua (left) and Afega Nomani (right). Ionatana Laulu (front) and several other teenagers line up in preparation for making their entry to the church (above).
'White Sunday' is actually a nickname for what was originally named 'Children's Sunday'.

Resplendent in her White Sunday finery, Milovale Tiatia follows the church service anxiously. Many weeks of practice have gone into this day, and her anxiety is understandable. Teachers from the church's Sunday School assist with the practices, rehearsals and during the performance, at which the children wear their best, often newly bought clothes.

The christening of Skye Sa'u during White Sunday celebrations at the Congregational Christian Church of Samoa, Grey Lynn (above). The Reverend Laau I. Tanielu holds the child beside the font, while parents May (holding Patrick) and Pati look on. Later (right) the Reverend Laau places his hand on the head of Uelese Tai, another member of his flock whom he has just christened.

Esera Leai delivers the sermon proudly during White Sunday, in accordance with the tradition that this is the one day that belongs to the young, a celebration of the children's witness to the gospel. On this day it is they who lead the prayers, recite verses from the Bible, perform plays for the adult congregation and, in Esera's case, deliver the word of God from the pulpit.

White Sunday includes even the very young. Here little Loana Vaaelua makes a speech for the congregation, assisted by her Sunday School teacher and watched over by a lineup of her impressed peers.

The youngest children of the Congregational Christian Church of Samoa, Grey Lynn, led by Sekone Fepulea'i (left hand raised), perform for their audience. Plays and recitations are an important part of White Sunday, and help instil self-confidence in the Samoan children, whose school teachers are often impressed by their ability at speaking and performing in public.

Milovale Tiatia (left) and her partner in drama, Masei Kovia, hold centre stage with their theatre piece, complete with Masei's visual aid (right).

The main formalities of White Sunday over for another year, the families of the congregation return to their homes for a formal family lunch. The young still hold pride of place at the dining table, however, and the food comprises a special meal in honour of the day. Taro, green bananas, chop suey, pisupo (corned beef), fried chicken, shellfish, tomatoes and fresh fruit are here laid out for the luncheon which the whole family enjoys. Later they will return to the church for the concluding service of Lotu Tamaiti, White Sunday.

Terai William (left) and Lucy Papa (right) decorate the hall in preparation for the hair-cutting ceremony for five-year-old Cook Island New Zealander, Kayne Lucas Upokokeu. Lucy is Kayne's grandmother, and she oversees preparations.

In the meantime, back at the family home (right), Kayne's hair is being tied into separate locks for the ceremony by his auntie, Tia Papa. It is usual for the women of the family to carry out this task.

Kayne's grandmother, Lucy, returns to help Tia to finish tying Kayne's hair into locks before they leave the house for the ceremony (above). An extended family occasion, it begins (right) with family prayers on Kayne's behalf, a moment of great solemnity. Kayne is seated in the place of honour, with his immediate family standing alongside him. His mother, Louisa, stands behind him and his father, Puna, is on her left. All guests wear Cook Islands eis – flower garlands – around their necks, and a tivaevae – an applique quilt – covers Kayne's 'throne'.

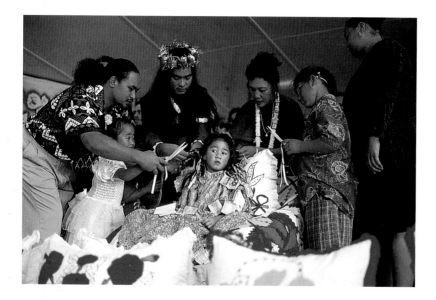

The hair cutting begins (above). As each lock of his hair is snipped, under the watchful eye of his family, Kayne is given a gift of money in return for the hair taken.

Kayne also has a congratulatory kiss bestowed upon him (below), while Lai Teiva takes her turn to snip a lock of Kayne's hair (right).
In accordance with the custom of the ceremony, the monetary contributions are accumulating on Kayne. These donations are very necessary, as it costs the family a considerable amount to host a hair-cutting ceremony.

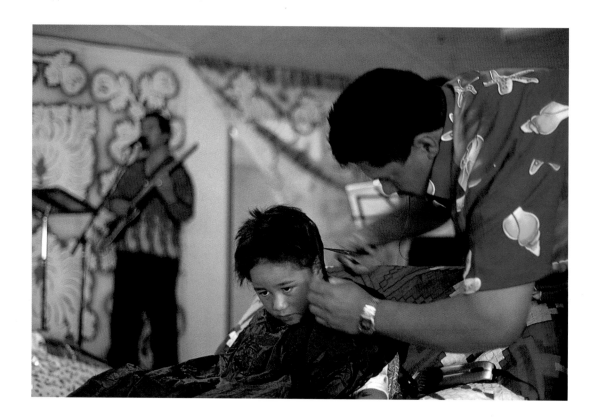

His hair cut short for the first time in his life, Kayne is given a necessary tidy-up by Ina Takairangi (above) before the next stage of the ceremony, while the guests are entertained by a Cook Islands band.

Freshly dressed, hatted and draped with eis, Kayne is escorted around the hall (right) by family patriarch Unakea Kauvai and Kayne's grandmother, Lucy Papa. To escort Kayne at this moment, in front of the assembled guests, is considered a great honour.

Reverend Tangaroa Uea, the family minister, leads the gathering in prayer (top). Then the feasting begins (bottom). For a Cook Islands banquet all courses, meat, fish, shellfish, vegetables, fruit, sweets and cakes are set out on the table and eaten together.

Kayne, the man of the moment, shorn of his locks, now gets down to some serious eating and soft drinking with his mates. Any food left uneaten at the end of the celebrations will be shared out and taken home by the guests.

Kayne's auntie Alana, his father's sister, and her daughter enjoy the feast in Kayne's honour. Whether in the Cook Islands or in New Zealand, the kopu tangata or extended family remains the foundation of all Cook Islands communities. Although often dispersed, the family will always be reunited for important social occasions such as hair-cutting ceremonies, 21st birthdays, weddings and funerals.

There are other aspects of the hair-cutting ceremony to come. Speech making, formal declarations of the day's importance, follows the feast. Here family matriarch Mama Vero (right) makes an impassioned speech before the guests on Kayne's behalf, with the boy enthroned again (centre) and other onlookers suitably impressed by Mama Vero's oratory.

The next stage of the hair-cutting ceremony, the O'ora, the giving of gifts, now begins (above). Guests come forward with contributions and place them before Kayne. Hand-sewn tivaevae quilts and pillows encased in tivaevae are popular gifts. And as no Cook Islands ceremony is complete without exuberant dancing, the gift-giving is accompanied by a dance performance (right) in front of Kayne, with Mama Vero Mistress of Ceremonies.

Now a man in the eyes of his family and friends, Kayne is called upon by Mama Vero to speak for himself. Covered in monetary donations, tivaevae gifts arrayed before him, he makes his speech to the assembly. Traditionally it was the oldest boy in the family who was accorded the hair-cutting ceremony, but today it is not unusual for all sons to be given one. All monetary donations are recorded and will be repaid when guests attend other families' hair-cutting ceremonies. His speech over, it remains only for Kayne to perform a Cook Islands dance (right) for his delighted family and friends.

Rites of Passage
Ear-piercing and Hair-cutting Ceremony of Niue

Remote, rugged and singularly beautiful, Niue Island is the world's largest raised coral atoll. Lifted aeons ago to an average of 50 m above the ocean by a convulsion in the earth's crust, Niue has no surrounding lagoon or surface streams and its fossilised coral core is covered by a very thin layer of soil. The island's jagged coastal cliffs are riddled with caves and crystal-clear rock pools, fed by underground springs. Around the island there is a sharp drop-off to unusually clear, deep ocean water, making Niue a scuba diver's nirvana. The waters also teem with game fish, notably wahoo, mahi mahi and tuna, which Niuean men catch from small, portable outrigger canoes. Niue also has the largest lowland tropical rainforest in the Pacific, a conservation area and a natural habitat for native pigeons, doves and fruit bats.

Niue was settled by people from Samoa and Tonga from about 1800 years ago, but over the last 30 years there has been considerable emigration. Severely limited employment opportunities on 'The Rock', as the island is affectionately known, have led to an exodus of Niueans, mainly to Auckland, but also to Wellington and Sydney, where jobs and higher educational opportunities are more readily available. Brave attempts have been made in recent years to establish a viable tourism industry on Niue, based on the island's distinctive natural attractions, to help stem the haemorrhage of people. However, these attempts have foundered, mainly because of unreliable airline connections with the outside world.

In Niuean expatriate communities such as Auckland's, the people hold fast to their traditional culture, including the important rites of passage for boys and girls, the hair-cutting and ear-piercing ceremonies. As in the Cook Islands, the hair cutting marked a Niuean youth's passing from boy-hood to manhood. But if a family had only daughters, an ear-piercing ceremony was performed instead, using a thorn from a lime bush to pierce the ear lobe. In recent times modifications have been made to this practice. Today in New Zealand, for example, modern instruments are used to pierce the girls' ears, as in the case of Gwenda Naepi (opposite). The Niuean name for ear piercing is huki teliga.

The ear-piercing and hair-cutting rituals are highly ceremonial occasions involving a great deal of planning and expense. Usually scheduled for a time when extended family members from Niue or Australia are able to attend, the ceremonies are accompanied by the presentation of gifts – money, household goods and foods such as taro, fish, pigs and lambs. The food gifts are divided up and shared out among the guests in accordance with the size of their financial contribution to the young people who are being honoured.

The Naepi family stands in prayer before the ear-piercing ceremony of 17-year-old Gwenda begins. She is flanked by her father Slaven (left) and mother Dahlia. Niuean girls can undergo the ear-piercing ceremony at any age from five to 18 years. Slaven and Dahlia Naepi decided that after having had hair-cutting ceremonies for their sons Clivenn and Gerald, it was only fair to have an ear-piercing ceremony for Gwenda, their only daughter.

The ear piercing takes place (right). While the lobe of Gwenda's left ear is penetrated with a sterilised needle, fingers are applied to the side of her head to comfort her. This modern method of ear piercing replaces the one traditionally used on Niue, whereby a thorn from a lime bush was pressed through the ear lobe, backed with a baby coconut.

The ear-piercing complete, the guests present Gwenda with gifts of money. Here her auntie, Fasala Nicolas, and her daughter Annie, present Gwenda with a lei made of notes. Gwenda's family spent $7000 on her ear-piercing ceremony, and collected $12,000 in return. The money donated at the ceremony will go towards Gwenda's tuition fees at university.

The lei of money is placed around Gwenda's neck (left). Then, one after another (right) guests come forward to congratulate Gwenda and present her with gifts, called in Niuean, Mena Fakalofa. These are usually items which will assist Gwenda in setting up a household of her own, such as embroidered bedspreads and pillows. Gwenda's dress is patterned in the traditional tapa designs of Niue.

Niuean boys, like their Cook Island counterparts, undergo a hair-cutting ceremony to mark their transition from boyhood to manhood. In Niuean this traditional rite of passage is called Hifiulu. Here Niuean brothers Tagamaka Talagi (13) and Alfie Talagi (15) proudly display their uncut locks before undergoing the hair-cutting ceremony.

Tagamaka and Alfie, dressed in a blend of modern and traditional Niuean costume, are blessed before the hair-cutting ceremony by the Reverend Talagi, a distinguished minister from Auckland's Niuean community. Like other South Pacific nations, Niue is strongly Christian and prayers precede all important cultural functions. The gospel was introduced to Niue by a Samoan-trained missionary, Peniamina, in 1846.

Tagamaka and Alfie, transformed after the Hifiulu ceremony, consider the difference in each other's appearance.

A Joyous Occasion
Tokelauan–Tuvaluan Wedding

The marriage of Makulu Siliga (bride) and Luka Tetau (groom) brings together two families from the remote island nations of Tuvalu and Tokelau. Held in the Nafanua Samoan Methodist Church, Avondale, by the Tokelauan Congregational Church, Auckland, the wedding is dignified with a blend of the rituals of both Tuvalu and Tokelau, Polynesian nations which lie to the north of Fiji and Samoa respectively. Dancing, gift-giving, speech-making and feasting are essential elements of Makulu and Luka's celebrations.

Mainly atolls barely above sea level, neighbouring nations Tuvalu and Tokelau are both threatened by rising sea levels as a result of global warming. Limited natural resources combined with a lack of educational and employment opportunities mean that migration to New Zealand from both island groups has been occurring over several decades. There are now significant Tokelauan communities in both Wellington and Auckland, while increasing out-migration from Tuvalu means that the Tuvaluan population in New Zealand is beginning to outnumber that of the Tokelauans.

Both the Tokelauan and Tuvaluan communities have held fast to their traditional cultures, in spite of Auckland being over 3000 km from their atoll homelands. The wedding of Makulu, who is of Tokelauan–Tuvaluan descent, and Luka, who is Tuvaluan, embodies the enduring strength of these two Polynesian cultures. Both nations being strongly Christian, the wedding is a devout occasion, witnessed by the wall hanging (opposite) which forms an imposing backdrop to the high table. The wedding cake on the right table is for the bride, the one on the left table is for the groom.

Luka and Makulu stand at the altar of the Nafanua Samoan Methodist Church, Avondale, Auckland, awaiting the beginning of the service (top). Beside Makulu is her father, who is giving the bride away.

A moment of great gravity, as the bride and groom exchange wedding vows at the altar under the direction of Minister Tui Sopoaga (left).

Before the wedding feast commences, Minister Tui Sopoaga (rear right) says grace from the high table. Following South Pacific custom, the bridal party is large, the wedding banquet lavish, the high table covered with Island foods and fresh fruit.

Backed by the band in full swing, Luka and Makulu await the beginning
of their wedding feast. Rising sea levels due to global warming mean
that the low-lying atolls of their homelands, Tokelau and Tuvalu, are now
environmentally threatened, causing many people such as Luka and Makulu
to seek lives of greater opportunity overseas.

A massive roast pig has pride of place as the wedding banquet is laid out.
In both Tuvalu and Tokelau, large pigs are roasted in umu (earth ovens), then
decorated with frangipani and hibiscus flowers. The pigs are then cut up and
divided into packs for the guests to take home, with smaller suckling pigs
being eaten at the feast itself.

Bedecked with monetary offerings from their guests, the newly wedded couple listen respectfully (left) to a speech in their honour by the mother of the bride, Pukipuki Tetau.

Both proud and shy, Luka and Makulu stand in front of their bridal party and guests before the gift-giving begins (above). The presents are piled in front of the wedding table in readiness for the next stage of the celebration.

79

The gift-giving is under way (top), in a ceremony called Faletuagane. This is done according to the traditional form of gift-giving on the main village of Tuvalu – Funafuti – and which has now been adopted by the other villages. The bride's uncle, Luta Gaualofa, presents her with a gift of mother-of-pearl shell (above). This shell is highly symbolic, representing as it does the sea as the main source of food for atoll nations and therefore symbolising life itself. Mother-of-pearl lures were traditionally used to catch tuna and bonito in Tuvalu and Tokelau.

A cousin of the bride, Tokai Panapa, performs a traditional dance in honour of the bride and groom.

The men begin to dance too. Here Fale Namoto performs a traditional solo dance, accompanied by his clapping comrades. Such spontaneous, joyful dancing is a wholly natural aspect of life on Tokelau and Tuvalu.

Now attired in their traditional costume, Makulu and Luka join in the dancing, called Fatele.

Luka and Makulu, now visibly more relaxed, enjoy their starring role as newly wed husband and wife, as well as displaying all the finery of their traditional Tokelauan–Tuvaluan costumes.

Honouring the Women
White Sunday in the Tongan Community

In Tongan communities White Sunday is known as Septima, which is the word for September in the Tongan language. Held over the last weekend in that month, Septima publicly acknowledges the work done for their congregations by the married and older women of the church. On that weekend the women dress entirely in white, to signify the purity of their relationship with God and their adherence to the gospel.

White Sunday actually begins on the Saturday morning of the Septima weekend. It is then that the women from the 13 branches of the Free Church of Tonga in Auckland gather at the church at 47 Favona Road, Mangere. Firstly a roll call is held, with the names of all the women present being called out in turn by the minister, beginning with the minister's wife. As each woman's name is read, she stands briefly before the congregation, so that everybody present can see her, then takes her seat again. After the roll call is complete the congregations return to their various branches for a feast, with the food being prepared and cooked by the men of the church. The women partake of the feast on their own. After all, this is the ladies' day! The feasting continues until late in the afternoon.

The following day, the last Sunday in September, the congregations gather in the various branches of their churches once again. Beginning at 11 am, they enjoy three or four hours of choral singing, interspersed with speeches by the ministers of the Free Churches of Tonga. Dressed in their best, Tongan women (right) gather at the Free Church of Tonga, Mangere, Auckland, for the celebration of Septima. Mele Kivalu (upper right, in glasses) sports a hat of spectacular design.

Ma'asi Hala, Meleoni Vehekite, Manu Mesake and Losena Filikitonga lead the congregation in prayer during the Septima celebrations.

Standing out as dramatically as a beacon amid a sea of white, sombrely dressed Eniketi Ta'i rises as her name is read out by the minister. Eniketi wears black to mark the recent loss of a loved one.

As the minister continues to call the roll of women present for Septima, each woman stands at the sound of her name, to be acknowledged for her work in the Tongan community. Here Tema Tu'i stands in answer to her name. The women wear white to symbolise the purity of their relationship with God.

Intoning their prayers, the Septima congregation close their eyes and join in the devotions. The Kingdom of Tonga is still one of the most devout Christian nations on earth, Tongan expatriate communities equally so. Today there are approximately 30,000 Tongan people living in New Zealand.

The very images of serenity and devotion, Sela Pulu
(above left) and Kalo Foleva (above), suppliants at the
Septima service at the Free Church of Tonga, Mangere,
personify the dedication of the women attending the
White Sunday service.

Suckling pigs are turn-roasted on spits like a sextet of didgeridoos, in preparation for the feast that is an essential feature of the Septima celebration. Roast pig is the most important ingredient in any Tongan banquet, the giving of pigs a meaningful tribute.

Done to a turn, a suckling pig sleeps peacefully among the other fare for the Septima feast, which includes salads, fish, crabs, corned beef, bread and fresh fruit.

Their devotions complete, now changed into informal dress, the women sit down to partake of the banquet prepared, cooked and served by the men of the Tongan community. This day, Septima, is the day that belongs to the women.

Schools on Show
Auckland Secondary Schools Maori and Pacific Islands Cultural Festival

The practices begin almost as soon as the new school year does. By February, at lunchtimes and in the evenings, the school grounds resonate with the sound of drums and song. By early March the pressure has intensified: costumes have been chosen and fitted, dance routines finely tuned, and the accompaniment perfected. All will be ready in time for the climax in late March, the three-day Auckland Secondary Schools Maori and Pacific Islands Cultural Festival held at the Manukau Sports Bowl, in Manukau City.

In its 26 years of existence the festival has grown to be the largest such event in the country, a celebration by Polynesian and Asian youth of their various cultures and one of the most colourful and exuberant events on Auckland City's calendar. From modest beginnings since its inception at Hillary College in 1976, the festival now involves over 162 cultural groups and a total of 13,000 students, from 52 schools across the whole Auckland region.

Performances take place on five well-spaced stages – Maori, Cook Islands, Niuean, Samoan and Tongan – and are continuous throughout the three days. There is a dazzling array of trophies to compete for, and standards of song, dance and accompaniment, particularly in the competitive sections, are extremely high. The winning groups bring great mana to their schools. Most importantly, the festival sustains the different cultures for the generations of young Pacific Island people born in New Zealand, as well as providing a visual and musical delight for the 100,000 people who come to watch. Preparation is everything (right). A Cook Islands Group from Otahuhu College attend to last minute costume adjustments in their changing tent before they take the stage for their festival performance.

For grease paint, read war paint. Students from Southern Cross Campus's Niuean Group adopt body paint to lend fearsomeness to their war dance (above).

Accompaniment is a vital part of each performance (top right). Mangere College's Cook Islands Group accompanists warm up in preparation for their performance, while (right), the Mangere College Cook Islands Group girls are costumed, relaxed and ready to dance.

A Mangere College boy strikes a casual pose before his festival group's performance. The woven coconut frond hat, ei (garland) and pareu (wraparound skirt) are all part of Cook Islanders' performance dress.

A Tongan performer, from De La Salle College, body oiled and war club
at the ready, prepares to take the stage. Festival judges award marks
for all aspects of a group's performance, including costume details.

A De La Salle College Samoan Group participant receives reassurance from one of his tutors. Weeks of preparation and practice reach their climax on the day of the performance, causing anxiety levels to rise. Competition between the different schools is intense during the three days of the festival performances, although there are non-competitive categories as well.

Deep breathing helps. Three Otahuhu College students do their best to relax before their group takes the stage. All these young performers are conscious that the eyes of their school, family, friends and community are upon them as they are on stage, an often nerve-wracking experience.

Some categories of performance in the Samoan competition are for boys only, some only girls, others are mixed. Here the faipese (conductor) of the Avondale College Samoan Group exudes a confident presence on stage during a boys' item. Each stage at the festival is decorated to reflect its home country's culture, in this case an iconic kava bowl and frangipani tapa patterns.

A pair of leading performers from Avondale College's Samoan Group happily attempt to upstage each other. Samoan cultural performances are noted for their flamboyance, exuberance and feats of athleticism from some dancers. New Zealand's 100,000-strong Samoan population – now mainly born here – is the largest Pacific Island community in the country.

Basking in the late summer sunshine, spectators await the beginning of the next performance (above). The festival draws an attendance of over 100,000 people over its three days.

Mangere College Cook Islands Group (left) perform a capa rima (action song), showing that the hands and hats, as well as the hips, contribute to the overall effect of their dance performance. Coconut bras are an essential fashion accessory.

Immaculately costumed, Marcellin College Samoan Group girls demonstrate their skills at the sasa, a traditional dance performed while seated. No fewer than 28 different schools had Samoan groups performing in the latest festival.

Girls from Mangere College Tongan Group perform the laka laka (above). Finely choreographed hand movements are a special feature of Tongan women's dancing. Traditionally, Tongan dances enact stories whose words are represented by hand and feet movements.

Performers from Mangere College Tongan Group in jocular mood on stage during their soke or stick dance (right). An important characteristic of their costume is the ta'ovala, the finely woven pandanus mats worn around the waist.

Aorere College Niuean Group boys perform a katoua, their ferocious club dance (left).

Girls from Otahuhu College's Niuean Group are in full voice (left). There are now 15 times more Niueans living in New Zealand than there are on Niue Island, so this festival is vitally important in maintaining the Niuean culture.

Members of the Southern Cross's Niuean Group check on
each other's movements as they perform their fia fia dance.

Maori, as tangata whenua – the indigenous people of New Zealand – play a prominent part in the festival. Here performers from Diocesan School present their whakaeke (entrance). The programme for the Maori section of the festival has a 'Female Groups Only' section, as well as sections for 'Male Groups Only' and co-educational schools.

The faces of 21st century Auckland. Diocesan girls, resplendent in Maori costume, radiate pleasure from being part of a performance group at the festival. Increased cultural interest and awareness is a secondary benefit of belonging to a Polynesian performance group.

A Te Wharekura o Hoana Waititi performer shows that warrior ferocity is not exclusive to male Maori dancers (above). Seen here performing a poi dance, the girls also wear the moko, the traditional Maori chin design.

A wheelchair warrior from Te Wharekura o Hoani Waititi Maori performance group shows indomitable courage as she performs the haka with the poi alongside her peers.

When the winners of each section of the festival performances are announced from the stage at the conclusion, exultation erupts from the supporters in the audience. Here students from McAuley High School (in blue uniform) greet the announcement of a winning performance with delight.

To the winners go the trophies. Schools compete keenly for the trophies awarded in each of the five cultural categories. After the aggregate winners are announced at the conclusion of the festival, there is great jubilation among the victors. Here a Samoan group of winners from St Dominic's College joins in the applause at their success.

Acknowledgements

Rev Tevita Afu, Sela and Latai Vailala, Vene, Dahlia and Gwenda Naepi, Ioane and Ianeta Iosua, Rev Tanielu and Litara Siliga, Bill Teriki, Papani and Sarah Tanu, Rev Laau and Ionie Tanielu, John and Amelia Tonga, Kelifi and Anne Lolofi Heimuli, Luka and Makulu Tetatau, Mama Vero, Lucy Joepapa, Louisa Papa and Puna Upokokeu, Joyce, Thomas, Alfie and Tanga Talangi, Robert Papa, Rev Toni Niuila and Hillary College.

EPSON®

Front cover
Luka Tetau (groom) and Makulu Siliga (bride) in traditional celebration costume after their wedding in the Nafanua Samoan Methodist Church.

Back cover
Kayne feasting after his hair-cutting ceremony.

Half title
Tongan White Sunday celebration at the Free Church of Tonga.

Title
The Atiuan Dancers at the Gluepot, 1992.

First published in 2002 by New Holland Publishers (NZ) Ltd
Auckland • Sydney • London • Cape Town

218 Lake Road, Northcote, Auckland, New Zealand
14 Aquatic Drive, Frenchs Forest, NSW 2086, Australia
86 Edgware Road, London W2 2EA, United Kingdom
80 McKenzie Street, Cape Town 8001, South Africa

www.newhollandpublishers.com

Copyright © 2002 in photography: Glenn Jowitt
Copyright © 2002 in text: Graeme Lay
Copyright © 2002 New Holland Publishers (NZ) Ltd

ISBN: 1 877246 53 0

Managing editor: Renée Lang
Design: Sally Hollis-McLeod, Moscow Design
Editor: Diana Harris
Cultural liaison and research: Glenn Jowitt

10 9 8 7 6 5 4 3 2 1

Colour reproduction by Microdot, Auckland, New Zealand
Printed by Toppan Printing Co., Hong Kong